SURVIVING

Earthquakes

Marne Ventura and
Heather Kissock

MEDIA ENHANCED BOOKS
AV2 BY WEIGL
ADDED VALUE • AUDIO VISUAL
www.av2books.com

Go to **www.av2books.com,** and enter this book's unique code.

BOOK CODE

AVQ42396

AV² by Weigl brings you media enhanced books that support active learning.

AV² provides enriched content that supplements and complements this book. Weigl's AV² books strive to create inspired learning and engage young minds in a total learning experience.

Your AV² Media Enhanced books come alive with...

Audio
Listen to sections of the book read aloud.

Key Words
Study vocabulary, and complete a matching word activity.

Video
Watch informative video clips.

Quizzes
Test your knowledge.

Embedded Weblinks
Gain additional information for research.

Slide Show
View images and captions, and prepare a presentation.

Try This!
Complete activities and hands-on experiments.

... and much, much more!

Published by AV² by Weigl
350 5th Avenue, 59th Floor
New York, NY 10118
Website: www.av2books.com

Library of Congress Cataloging-in-Publication Data
Names: Ventura, Marne, author.
Title: Earthquakes / Marne Ventura.
Description: New York, NY : AV2 by Weigl, [2019] | Series: Surviving | Audience: Grade 4 to 6. | Includes index.
Identifiers: LCCN 2018053479 (print) | LCCN 2018054320 (ebook) | ISBN 9781489697837 (Multi User ebook) | ISBN 9781489697844 (Single User ebook) | ISBN 9781489697813 (hardcover : alk. paper) | ISBN 9781489697820 (softcover : alk. paper)
Subjects: LCSH: Earthquakes--Juvenile literature.
Classification: LCC QE521.3 (ebook) | LCC QE521.3 .V47 2019 (print) | DDC 363.34/95--dc23
LC record available at https://lccn.loc.gov/2018053479

Printed in the United States of America in Brainerd, Minnesota
1 2 3 4 5 6 7 8 9 0 22 21 20 19 18

122018
120118

Project Coordinator: Heather Kissock   Designer: Ana María Vidal

Every reasonable effort has been made to trace ownership and to obtain permission to reprint copyright material. The publishers would be pleased to have any errors or omissions brought to their attention so that they may be corrected in subsequent printings.

Weigl acknowledges Getty Images, iStock, and Alamy as its primary image suppliers for this title.

First published by The Child's World in 2016.

Earthquakes

Contents

Chapter 1

Many homes in Port-au-Prince were not well built. This is one reason the earthquake caused so much damage.

The Earth Is Moving!

Evans Monsignac sold his last batch of rice. It was a Tuesday afternoon. He was finishing his day at a market in Port-au-Prince, Haiti. Suddenly, the ground started to shake. Goods flew through the air. Monsignac fell to the ground. Buildings started to fall down around him. A big piece of concrete landed over where he lay. It blocked out the light. Eventually, the ground stopped shaking. Monsignac was alive but trapped.

The January 2010 earthquake in Haiti lasted only 40 seconds. But it caused a lot of damage. Many buildings and homes were turned into **rubble**. Dust and smoke covered Port-au-Prince in a dark cloud.

After the quake, Monsignac was afraid to move. He feared the concrete above him would fall if he tried to get out. He heard people yelling for help around him. No one came to dig him out. After about a day, it was quiet.

About 300,000 people died in the earthquake. More than a million others lost their homes. People looked for survivors in the ruined city for weeks. It would take years to clean up and rebuild.

After 27 days, someone finally found Monsignac. He had lost 60 pounds (27 kilograms). He had bad sores on his arms. But he was alive. He had survived by drinking dirty water that came down to him. He was the last person found alive in the rubble.

What Causes an Earthquake?

Earth's surface is made up of huge pieces called **tectonic plates**. Imagine tapping a hard-boiled egg against a table. The cracked pieces of the shell are like the plates that cover Earth. Sometimes, two plates bump into each other and stick. Energy builds. The edges of the plates finally slip apart. This makes **seismic waves** that shake the ground. Earthquakes happen near the **faults** between plates.

The 2010 Haiti earthquake was a rare disaster. Scientists estimate that about 1.5 million earthquakes shake the ground each year. But most are too small to feel. Monsignac could not know that a big quake would strike that day in the market. But he did not give up when he found himself in a hard situation. He did what he needed to do to survive an earthquake.

Many people in Haiti lived in camps after the earthquake. One camp was at a small airport.

The 2011 earthquake that struck Japan caused more than **$235 billion** in damages.

The scale used to measure earthquake strength was created in **1935**.

About **50,000** earthquakes each year can be detected **without** instruments.

Chapter 2

Learning the Risks

Earthquakes alone do not usually hurt people. For example, someone playing in an open field during a quake will probably not be injured. But earthquakes can make buildings fall. They can cause fires. They might block roads. Water and food might not be usable after a quake. These things make earthquakes dangerous.

When earthquakes destroy roads or railways, it can make it difficult for emergency responders to provide relief.

Eric Clark was six years old when an earthquake hit his hometown of Anchorage, Alaska, in 1964. He was watching a show on his family's new television when the quake hit. The TV fell onto the floor. The kitchen cupboards opened. Boxes and cans flew out. Eric and his family left their home. The house swayed and shook. Eric's dad shut off the power and gas to the house. Eric watched a tree in the backyard split down the middle.

Big earthquakes like the one that hit Anchorage can cause lots of damage to stationary objects. It is important to know the risks so you can stay safe.

Some emergency responders use rescue dogs. These dogs can help find people in disasters.

If people get caught in the rubble of a destroyed structure, they should not panic. They should try to signal their location. But you can lose your voice and tire yourself out by yelling. There are other ways to signal for help. Some people use objects to make noise. For example, you could tap a loose pipe every few minutes.

Earthquakes cause other dangers, too. Some are invisible. Broken pipes can leak gas. Gas can explode near a flame. Eric Clark's dad was smart to turn off the gas. If a wall or door feels hot, there might be fire on the other side. Stay away from the flames. You can protect yourself from smoke by putting a wet cloth over your mouth and nose.

How Do Earthquakes Cause Tsunamis?

In March 2011, a big earthquake shook Japan. The six-minute quake was strongest in the ocean. Huge waves rose up and raced toward shore. The **tsunami** traveled at nearly 500 miles (805 kilometers) per hour. It grew to a height of about 130 feet (40 meters). It caused a lot of damage when it reached land. Tsunamis occur when tectonic plates on the ocean floor rise or fall suddenly. The movement makes the water above speed away in a rolling wave.

In 2014, an earthquake in Napa, California, caused more than 30 water main breaks.

Earthquakes can also cause flooding if they break pipes or dams. Moving water that is even a few inches (centimeters) deep can knock you off your feet. Also, chemicals like cleaning supplies can get into the water. These can be bad to touch or inhale. If there is unclean water that is not moving, you can make a bridge out of boxes or boards and use it to cross over. Otherwise, do not try to cross on foot. Officials will let you know when tap water is safe to use. Use bottled water until then.

Some earthquakes cause the power to go out. If this happens, refrigerated food starts to go bad after about a day. People should eat canned or dried food if they cannot get fresh food. Phones, televisions, and computers will stop working without power. You can listen to a battery-operated radio to stay connected. Officials often use the radio to send information during and after disasters.

Major damage can occur after an earthquake, too. Hours after the 1964 Anchorage earthquake, tsunamis hit Oregon and California. The waves killed 16 people. There were also **aftershocks** in the following days. Clark and his family slept in their living room after the quake. They did not want to get separated if the aftershocks caused more damage.

Timeline

People have recorded earthquakes for thousands of years. Some of these earthquakes have resulted in large amounts of damage or caused many deaths.

132 AD The first seismoscope, a device used to detect earthquakes, is created in China.

1906 A **magnitude** 7.9 earthquake strikes San Francisco, California, causing a series of fires. In total, more than 28,000 buildings are destroyed.

1960 The largest recorded earthquake in history strikes Chile. The resulting tsunami creates waves more than 30 feet (10 m) high.

1976 The Chinese city of Tangshan is struck by an earthquake that kills more than 240,000 people and destroys 85 percent of the city's buildings.

2010 The country of Haiti is struck by an earthquake that kills hundreds of thousands of people. More than one third of the nation's population is affected by the earthquake.

2018 An earthquake strikes the city of Palu, in Indonesia, killing more than 2,000 people. Government officials expect that recovery and rebuilding will take more than two years.

Chapter 3

Organizations such as the International Search and Rescue Advisory Group (INSARAG) take part in earthquake response simulations to help test emergency response methods.

Making a Plan

Do you wear a helmet when you ride a bike? How about a seatbelt in the car? Your bike or car may never crash. But it is good to be safe. A plan is like a helmet or a seatbelt. You may never need it. But if there is a big quake, having a plan can keep you and your family safe.

Where will you go if an earthquake happens? A safe place will protect you from falling or flying objects. Beneath a table or desk is good. But stay away from windows, kitchen cabinets, and bookshelves.

People who are not at home when a quake hits have other challenges. It is best to be in an open area if you are outdoors when a quake hits. Stay away from buildings, power lines, and trees. Buildings and trees can hurt you when they fall. Power lines can shock or burn.

Families should plan how they will get in touch after an earthquake. Pick a place to meet. Local parking lots or parks are good choices. Families should also think about how to contact each other. Each family member can keep a card with important phone numbers and meeting places in a backpack or notebook. It's also good to memorize your family members' phone numbers.

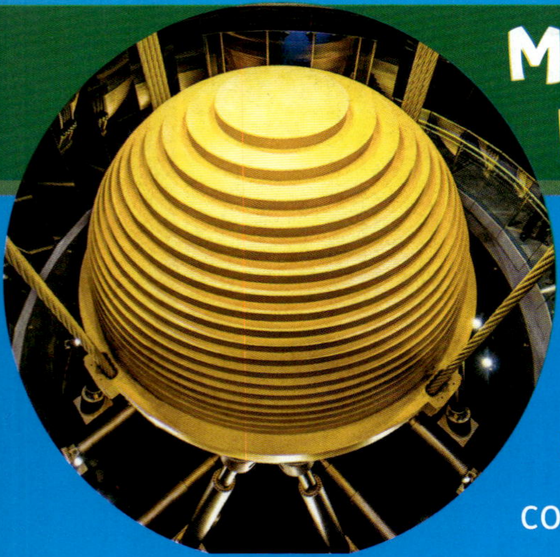

Making Buildings Earthquake-Proof

Engineers are getting better at making buildings that will not fall down when the ground shakes. Homes made of bricks or blocks are most likely to collapse in an earthquake. When a house shakes sideways, the blocks come apart. The roof falls in. Engineers are learning how to make walls that can move back and forth without breaking. Modern builders tie the walls, floor, roof, and base into a strong box that holds together during movement.

After you make a plan, you need to know when to use it. How do you know when an earthquake is happening? Sometimes, there is a rumble that starts soft and gets louder. The walls and windows might shake. The ground might move like a wave under your feet. It may be hard to stand or move. It is important to know what you will do so you can act quickly.

There are also ways to prepare your house. Adults can bind tall bookshelves to the wall. They can move heavy wall hangings away from beds and couches. That way, objects will not fall in a way that hurts someone if the house shakes.

About **100** earthquakes cause damage **each year**.

Alaska has more earthquakes than **any other U.S. state**.

The **deepest** earthquakes take place about **400 miles** (750 km) below Earth's surface.

Chapter 4

A family's emergency kit should have enough supplies for at least three days.

Creating a Kit

On a normal day, you get water from the kitchen faucet. The refrigerator keeps your food fresh. You turn on the heater if you are cold. Electric lights let you see in the dark. If you get hurt, someone takes you to the doctor.

When a big earthquake happens, it may take a day or more for workers to restore electricity and water and clear the roads. Having a kit with supplies can help you survive if an earthquake turns a normal day into an emergency.

Think about what you and your family will need if an earthquake hits. Store your supplies in sturdy, waterproof bags or buckets with handles. Put them on a low shelf in your garage or on the floor of a closet. This way, they will not fall if the ground shakes. Make sure everyone in your family knows where the supplies are.

How Are Earthquakes Measured?

Scientists measure the magnitude of a quake using a **seismograph**. It has a pen that hangs over a rotating drum covered with paper. When the earth shakes, the pen makes marks on the paper. A long line with deep wiggles shows a big earthquake. A short line with shallow wiggles shows a small earthquake. The largest recorded earthquake magnitude in the world occurred in Chile on May 22, 1960.

You may not be able to get to your emergency supplies during an earthquake. You may need to leave your home. A small kit with water, food, and first-aid supplies in the trunk of your family car will come in handy if you cannot get to your big kit.

It may seem like the threat of an earthquake would make people want to avoid living in areas where quakes happen most often. But many people live with the risk of earthquakes every day. They do not worry because they know that big earthquakes are rare. And if one does happen, they know they will be prepared to survive.

EMERGENCY KIT CHECKLIST

- ☐ 3 gallons (11 liters) of bottled water per person
- ☐ Canned and dried food to last three days
- ☐ Hand-operated can opener
- ☐ Battery-operated radio
- ☐ Flashlight
- ☐ Extra batteries
- ☐ First-aid kit
- ☐ Whistle
- ☐ Dust mask, plastic sheets, and duct tape
- ☐ Moist towelettes, trash bags, and ties
- ☐ Wrench or pliers
- ☐ Local maps
- ☐ Special medications or eyeglasses
- ☐ Baby or pet supplies
- ☐ Sleeping bags
- ☐ Set of clothing with sturdy shoes for each person
- ☐ Fire extinguisher

Earthquake Tracking

While earthquakes take place all around the world, they are most likely to occur on the edges of major tectonic plates. These spots are monitored by various groups so that warnings can be issued when necessary.

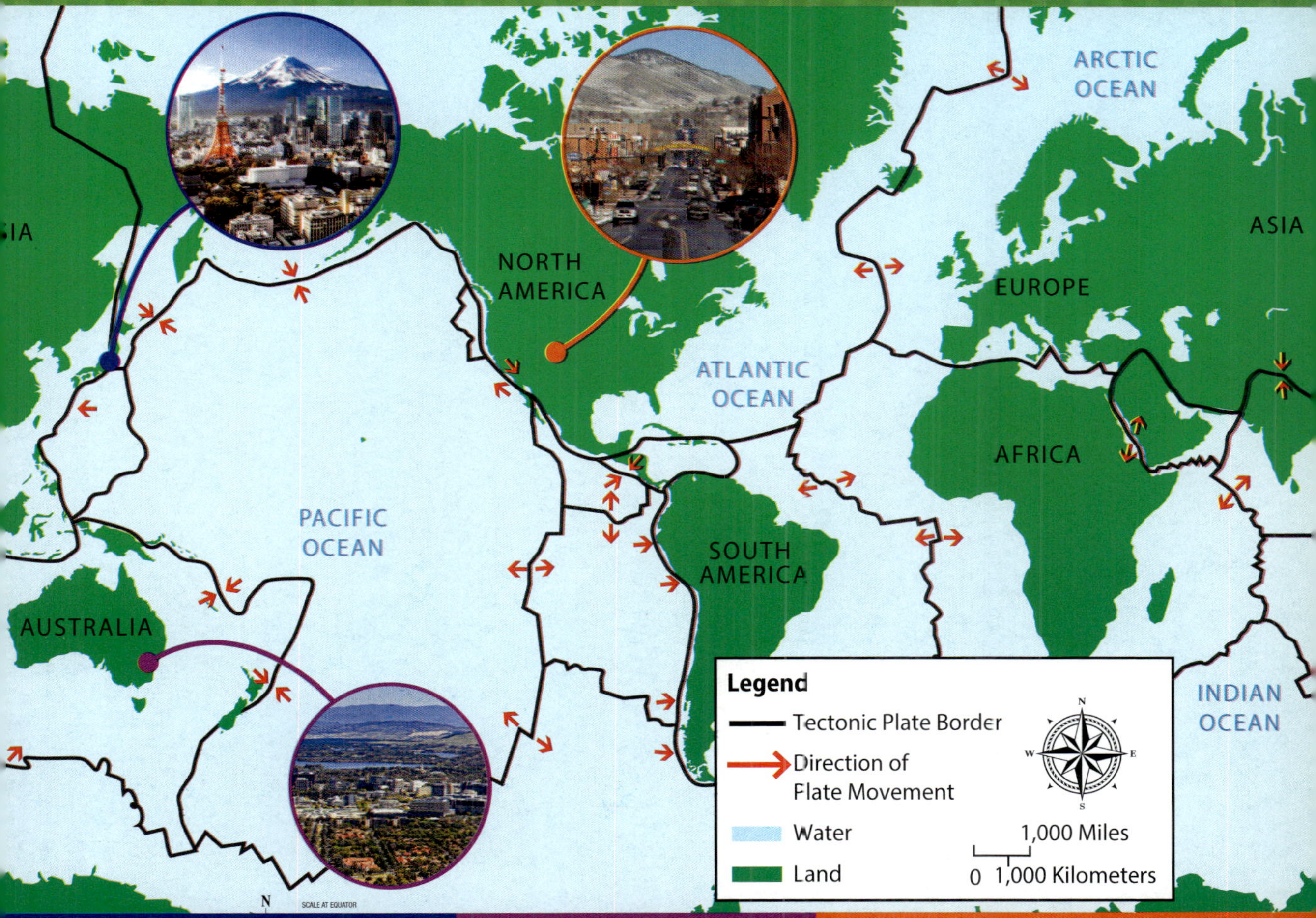

Japan Headquartered in Tokyo, the Japan Meteorological Agency provides earthquake information to the government in order to help it respond to disasters properly.

Australia Geoscience Australia is a government organization that monitors and reports on earthquakes. It uses data from more than 300 stations around the world.

United States The National Earthquake Information Center (NEIC) is based in Golden, Colorado. It monitors earthquakes around the world, locating about 30,000 each year.

Quiz

1 How many earthquakes cause damage each year?

2 How long did the January 2010 earthquake in Haiti last?

3 What is INSARAG?

4 What percent of Tangshan's buildings were destroyed during a 1976 earthquake?

5 How can earthquakes cause flooding?

6 What does a seismograph measure?

7 What makes up Earth's surface?

8 Where is the National Earthquake Information Center (NEIC) based?

ANSWERS **1.** About 100 **2.** 40 seconds **3.** The International Search and Rescue Advisory Group **4.** 85 **5.** By breaking pipes or dams **6.** The magnitude of an earthquake **7.** Tectonic plates **8.** Golden, Colorado

Key Words

aftershocks: small earthquakes that come after the main quake. Aftershocks get smaller as more time passes after the quake.

engineers: experts at designing buildings or machines. Engineers design buildings to be strong enough to withstand earthquakes.

faults: cracks between two tectonic plates in the earth's surface. Earthquakes occur near faults.

magnitude: a measurement of the size of an earthquake. Earthquakes with magnitude 5.5 and greater cause damage.

rubble: piles of broken stones and bricks. Being trapped under rubble is dangerous.

seismic waves: vibrations in Earth's crust caused by earthquakes. Scientists measure seismic waves to find an earthquake's magnitude.

seismograph: a device used to measure vibrations in the earth's crust. Seismograms are reports made by seismographs during an earthquake.

tectonic plates: pieces of Earth's crust that move slowly. Earthquakes occur in the faults between tectonic plates.

tsunami: a large, destructive wave. Tsunamis are caused by earthquakes.

Index

Log on to www.av2books.com

AV² by Weigl brings you media enhanced books that support active learning. Go to www.av2books.com, and enter the special code found on page 2 of this book. You will gain access to enriched and enhanced content that supplements and complements this book. Content includes video, audio, weblinks, quizzes, a slide show, and activities.

AV² Online Navigation

Book Pages
AV² pages directly correspond to pages in the book.

Audio
Listen to sections of the book read aloud.

Video
Watch informative video clips.

Embedded Weblinks
Gain additional information for research.

Key Words
Study vocabulary, and complete a matching word activity.

Try This!
Complete activities and hands-on experiments.

Quizzes
Test your knowledge.

Slide Show
View images and captions, and prepare a presentation.

AV² was built to bridge the gap between print and digital. We encourage you to tell us what you like and what you want to see in the future.

Sign up to be an AV² Ambassador at www.av2books.com/ambassador.

Due to the dynamic nature of the Internet, some of the URLs and activities provided as part of AV² by Weigl may have changed or ceased to exist. AV² by Weigl accepts no responsibility for any such changes. All media enhanced books are regularly monitored to update addresses and sites in a timely manner. Contact AV² by Weigl at 1-866-649-3445 or av2books@weigl.com with any questions, comments, or feedback.